MARBLING ON FABRIC

ANNE CHAMBERS

SEARCH PRESS

First published in Great Britain 1995

Search Press Limited
Wellwood, North Farm Road,
Tunbridge Wells, Kent TN2 3DR

ISBN 0 85532 788 X

If you have difficulty in obtaining any of the
materials or equipment mentioned in this
book, please write for further information to
the Publishers.
    Search Press Limited
    Wellwood, North Farm Road
    Tunbridge Wells, Kent TN2 3DR
    England

*For Theodore, from his
loving grandmother.*

Printed in Spain by Elkar S. Coop, Bilbao 48012

*Right: China silk square scarf by Polly Fox,
marbled with acrylic colours on a bath of caragheen.*

CONTENTS

INTRODUCTION

Although a lot is known of the history and techniques of marbling on paper, and there are now many books on the subject, marbling on fabric is a comparatively new art which is not, as yet, widely practised. The only early mention is by the nineteenth-century marbler C.W. Woolnough, who wrote of a brief period of marbling on bookcloth, which for various reasons came to nothing. The Japanese also marbled with indigo on kimonos. In this century, Pete Carr and Georgie Downes marbled lengths of cloth in the late sixties, which were made into fashionable shirts by Mr Fish. Some fairly simple marbling was, and still is, done in India, and in Turkey fine marbled silk is made into beautiful ties and scarves in a town called Bursa.

The great advantage of marbling is that one requires no skill as an artist. The paints are lightly dropped on a tray of liquid (the bath) and then these colours can be gently swirled into marvellous fluid patterns with, say, a knitting needle or pencil (the stylus). Then the fabric is very carefully laid on the surface of the bath, so that the pattern is transferred to it.

It is not really possible to make the diversity of patterns which you can make when marbling on paper, nor is it really necessary, since the material itself lends interest in its colour, texture and shine, which paper does not have. However, quite a variety of designs can be made.

They are roughly divided into two kinds. The first involves random dropping or spattering of colours on the bath, while the second involves putting down your colours in the traditional way, drop by drop, fairly evenly across the bath. You can drop the different colours alongside each other, or symmetrically on top of each other, then run a stylus through them in different ways.

With the recent advent of really good fabric paints, it can be quite a simple process. Of course, as with any other art form, it is possible to extend your skills, so that you can get even better and richer effects, but you can make a start very simply, with just a few basic materials. Even if you have never marbled before, you should very quickly be able to achieve some immediate and very pretty results. The first section of this book is devoted to using ordinary fabric paints on cotton, then we will move on to more advanced techniques and different fabrics, marbling with acrylic paints, and then marbling with oil paints. This last process is equally easy, just messier!

HOW TO BEGIN

MATERIALS

• Something big enough to marble your squares of fabric in, such as a 7.5cm (3in) deep roasting tin, square washing-up bowl, plastic cat-litter tray or seed box – any of these will do to use as your 'bath'.

• Newspapers to cover your work surface, to keep it clean from splashes of paint.

• Four small pots or old cups to hold your colours.

• Knitting needle or pencil to use as a stylus to swirl your paints on the surface of the bath.

• Some clean, washed pieces of cotton such as old sheets or pillowcases, T-shirts, or even jeans, cut into squares for marbling.

• Three small jars of fabric paint from an art or craft shop, or the fabric department of a large store. These are special water-based paints with an additive which makes them float on the surface of your bath. Some fabric paints work better for marbling than others – I found the German ones very good. Do not try to mix different brands, as the ingredients are not always the same.

It is better to buy three primary colours, as these can be mixed to make other colours as well. Get a good deep blue, a strong yellow, and a red which is deep scarlet rather than pillar-box red.

• Four cheap paintbrushes about 6mm (¼in) wide.

• A packet of cellulose wallpaper paste, or a box of ordinary household laundry starch from a supermarket or grocer's.

• The picture below also shows other things you may like to acquire at some point, such as combs, bamboo brushes for spattering, and other paints.

A selection of some of the things you will need for marbling on fabric.

MARBLING — STEP BY STEP

1 Mix up your wallpaper paste or starch according to the directions on the packet in a plastic bucket, and leave it on one side. Both these mixtures work better if left to rest and settle for a short time before you use them. If your work surface is not tiled or easy-clean, protect it by covering it with newspaper.

2 Now mix up your paints: put a teaspoon of each of the fabric paints into one of the pots or cups. It will be quite thick, because its original purpose was for painting on fabric. Add, very slowly from a jug or old teapot, enough cold water to make it more liquid, stirring it all the time with one of the paintbrushes. When it is liquid enough to drop easily off your brush, it should be ready for use. Test the colours on your bath – they should spread satisfactorily and not clump up. Skim your test drops off with a strip of newspaper before starting to marble.

3 Cut up your cloth into squares, making sure that they are not too big to fit neatly into the bath, leaving a margin of about 2.5cm (1in) all round.

Cut up some of the newspapers into strips wide enough to skim the bath (to clean it) and some large squares the size of the bath, to lay down for the same purpose. Put these alongside your work surface, and have a plastic bag or bin in a convenient place to hold the used newspaper strips and squares.

4 Add enough warm water to your wallpaper paste or starch to make it the consistency of thin cream; it should not feel thick when you put your hand in it, but quite fluid. Then pour it slowly into the bath, and line up your pots of paints with the brushes in them alongside. You are now ready to begin!

5 Take a strip of newspaper just wider than your bath (so that you can get right to the edges) and skim the surface of the bath to remove any bubbles. Then either leave the paper neatly tucked up against the far end of your bath or throw it into your plastic container. This is always the first step every time you intend to marble something.

6 Gently drop one of the colours on to the surface of the bath. It should spread out: if it does not, the paint is probably too thick, and needs thinning with a little more water, after which you should stir the paint well.

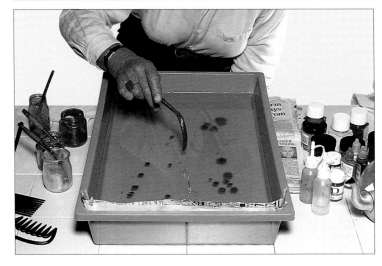

7 When the colour spreads properly, drop on your next colour. You will find that the first colour will have spread into such a thin film that you can hardly see it.

8 If the second colour works, drop on your third. At this stage, a random arrangement of drops of colour will be fine.

9 Now lay your piece of fabric down on to the surface of the bath, very smoothly, patting it gently to make sure no air bubbles have been trapped beneath it.

10 Lift off the fabric. You will find that the pattern on the surface of the bath has transferred itself to the fabric.

11 Rinse it carefully (the paint is not yet quite set so do not rub or scrub or you may smear the pattern) with cold water poured from a jug.

12 Finally, either lay the fabric flat on newspaper to dry or hang it on a convenient rail or line, with some newspaper underneath to catch the drips.

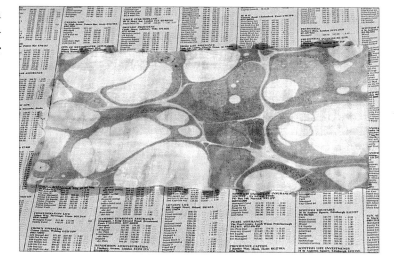

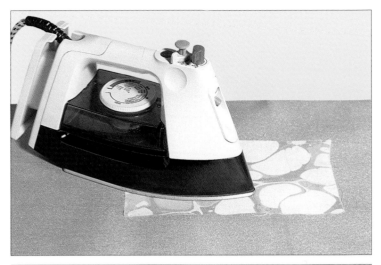

13 When the material is nearly dry, iron it on the back with a very hot iron to help set the colour.

If your marbling has been less than perfect, do not be discouraged – remember that you will certainly improve with practice.

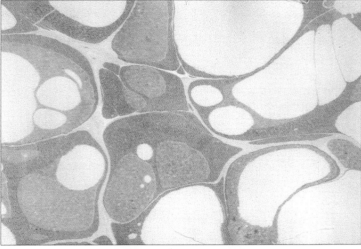

14 The finished square shows how effective even the simplest random 'pebble' pattern can look.

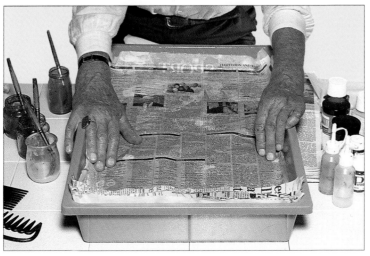

CLEANING UP

To clean the bath, lay a piece of newsprint on the surface of the bath to pick up any remaining floating paint.

Cleaning up when you have finished your marbling session is easy, because the colours are water-based, so the pots and brushes can be washed in hot water and detergent. Rinse very carefully, because remaining traces of detergent on your brushes or in your pots would affect your colours the next time you wanted to marble.

DIFFERENT PATTERNS

A STYLUSED PATTERN

1 Follow exactly the same procedure as you did above, except that when you get to stage 8, before you lay the fabric down, use a stylus (a knitting needle or pencil) to stir the colours gently into a swirling pattern, following the direction shown in the diagram. Do not do this too roughly, or the colours will sink! Always remember that they are only a thin film floating on the surface of the water, and that you have to move carefully.

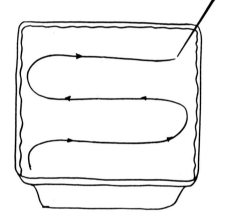

2 Lay down your fabric on the bath just as you did in stage 9.

3 Now pick it up – and admire a completely different pattern created from the same colours as you used before.

Finish off by rinsing and drying the fabric as you did before.

4 The strokes of the stylus in different directions create this distinctive pattern.

SPATTERING

This is another idea using random drops. It works very well when marbling fabric, especially silks and satins. Here the colours are thrown or splattered on by charging a long stiff-bristled brush such as a pastry brush or baby's bottle brush with colour and then knocking it against the side of your hand or a stick of wood to shower the surface of the bath with drops. (This can be a bit messy, so make sure the surrounding surfaces are well protected by newspaper.)

Sometimes the last colour can have an additive (see page 25) to make it move differently from the other colours; sometimes the additive is diluted with water but no colour and sprinkled lightly over the colours at the end. This can also be done with an atomiser. As before, experimenting is great fun, but try to make a note of what you have done, so that you can repeat a good piece of marbling another time.

The same dropped-on colours can also, of course, be combed (see page 18), or combed and then stylused.

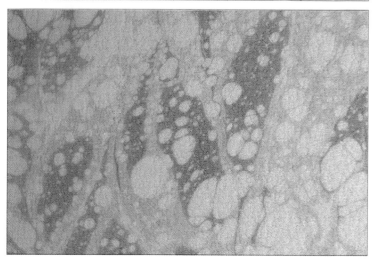

HEARTS

1 For a different look, instead of dropping the colours on to the surface at random, drop them in an orderly fashion, in lines across your bath, one colour on top of another. Here I am starting with blue.

2 Next, drop red on top of the blue. (The first colour tends to spread out very thinly without other colours to push against it, so at this stage it will be an almost invisible film on the surface of the bath.)

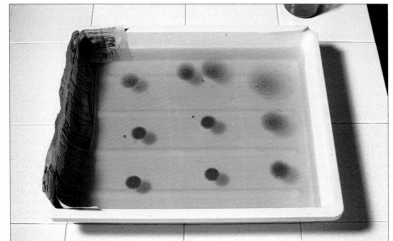

3 Now drop yellow in the middle of each drop as well (see the diagram).

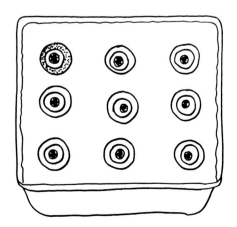

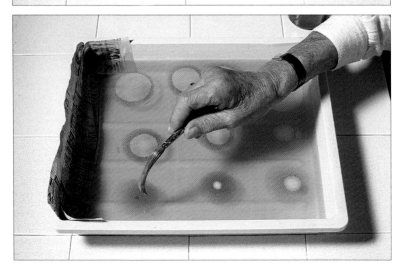

4 Next, draw your stylus carefully through each drop, making it heart-shaped (see the diagram). You can draw your stylus up and down, or across – the pattern variations are endless.

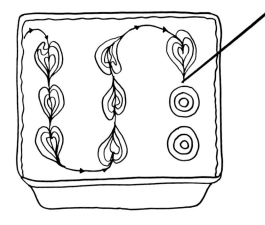

5 The finished design shows a clear heart-shaped pattern.

SWIRLS

1 This is another 'controlled' pattern. Drop your colours in rows across your bath, one colour in each row. Here, again, I am starting with blue.

2 Next, place a row of red drops in between the blue ones.

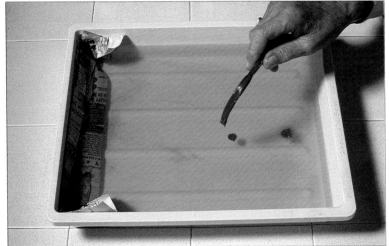

3 Drop on rows of yellow this time. Now carry on adding more colour so that there is plenty on the surface of the bath by the time you have finished.

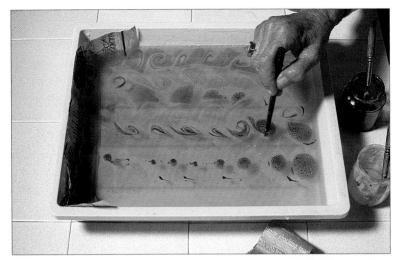

4 Next, use your stylus to make each drop into a separate individual swirl, each of a different colour.

5 Carefully lay down your fabric on the surface of the bath, then remove, rinse and dry it as usual.

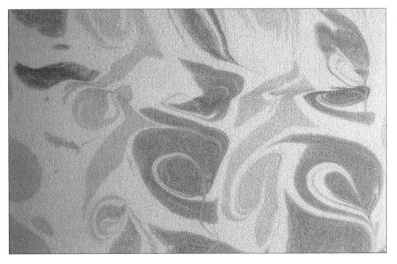

6 The finished pattern.

17

COMBING

1 You can collect a great variety of combs: garden or table forks, hair combs, Afro combs, or combs made with pins or nails expressly to fit your bath. Or get a coarse plastic comb, break off alternate teeth so that the remaining ones are widely set, and comb through your colour with that. All these combs give different effects.

First of all, put down streaks – not drops – of your first colour. I am starting with red this time.

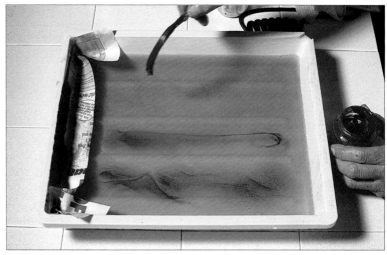

2 Now add streaks of blue in between the rows of red.

3 Finish off with streaks of yellow. By now the surface of the bath should be fully covered with colour.

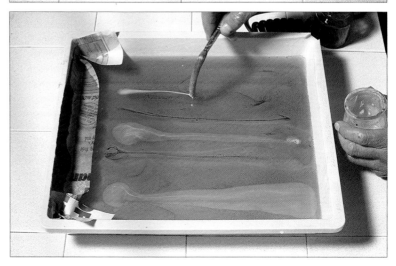

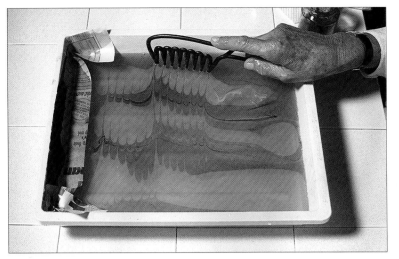

4 Now comb at right angles to the streaks of colour. As with stylusing, you should move the comb very lightly, and only just enough to comb the pattern – do not drag the teeth deeply through the bath. You will find you get better at this with practice.

Colours can also be combed and then stylused.

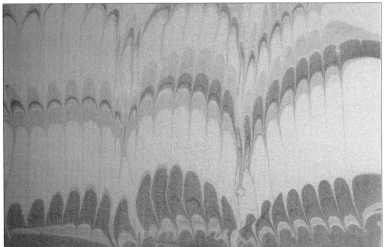

5 This elegant pattern has the look of classic marbling.

6 Using a finer-toothed comb will give quite a different effect, producing a subtle fine-grained pattern.

To get a greater variety of colour, you can mix up your primaries – the blue, red and yellow – as follows:

Blue + yellow = green
Blue + red = purple
Yellow + red = orange

These can be made different again by adding more or less of the second colour. You can get every range of green, for example, from olive green to deep racing green, by altering the amount of yellow you add to the blue.

THINGS TO MAKE

These pieces of fabric can be used for a variety of purposes. You can use them as denim squares for patching or decorating jeans, or fringe the edges to make table mats, or join them all together to make a patchwork skirt, throwover or cushion cover. They are also perfect for making a patchwork quilt (see pages 34–35). Or make them into hair scrunchies, lavender bags, padded coathangers, greetings cards, glasses cases, hairbands, slides, pencil cases…

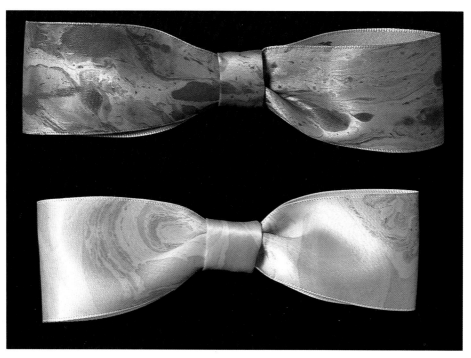

Decorative bows.

MORE ADVANCED TECHNIQUES

You may have found that the colours of your marbled fabric are not as deep as you would like. (Using the same method, but using oil paints instead of fabric paints, will produce a deeper effect (see page 28)).

In this section I will explain how to deepen the colours still using fabric paints, and also how to do rather more advanced techniques, using different additives and dispersants.

Basically, the method of marbling is always the same: you drop colours on to the surface of the bath and manipulate them into a pattern of some kind, which is then taken up by the material which you gently lay down on it.

However, you can now extend your range by trying out more advanced techniques and new materials.

FABRICS

You do not have to stick to cotton, as most fabrics can be marbled satisfactorily. All the cottons and linens, most synthetics such as polyester and polyester/cotton, satins, and silk (both pure silk and synthetic) take the colours well. Some fabrics, however, do not – I have never had any success with wool, textured material such as corduroy, and unbleached calico (I hoped this would be very interesting but as it turned out, it refused to take the colour at all!).

You should wash all these materials with a mild detergent before marbling, to remove any size remaining in the fabric after it has been manufactured. (Pure silk is the exception to this rule, as no size is used in its manufacture.)

When you have washed and dried the materials, you should treat them with a solution of alum, which will make them more receptive to the marbling colours. The technical term for this is mordanting (from the Latin *mordere*, meaning 'to bite'), and refers to a substance used to fix textile dyes. This treatment will give you much deeper colours than in the previous chapter, when you were simply marbling with washed cotton, and the colours will be more permanent.

To make up the mordant solution, buy a packet of powdered alum (100g (4oz)) from a chemist/drugstore, and dissolve this by adding it to 1 litre (2 pints/1 quart) of cold water and boiling it up in a saucepan. When the crystals are completely dissolved, put the solution in a container or plastic bucket big enough to take the fabric. Soak the fabric for five minutes or so in the solution, then wring it out, and hang it up to dry. Do not forget to iron it before marbling, so that it is quite smooth and has no creases in it.

Remnants of material can be bought quite cheaply, and charity and thrift shops are a good source of materials. Do not reject fabric, or articles, which are sound but faded or shabby; I once made a set of very pretty Easter table mats from some very unpromising old yellow rep curtains which had been badly faded by the sun. Odd lengths of satin ribbon can also be bought quite cheaply, and make very attractive book-marks, or ties: excellent small presents.

As before, all your fabrics must be ironed on the back with as hot an iron as the fabric will allow, when nearly dry, to set the colour. This can also be done in a tumble-drier set at the appropriate heat, on a cycle of fifty minutes.

THE BATH

METHYL CELLULOSE PASTE

It is well worth while looking for a methyl cellulose wallpaper paste, rather than just an ordinary cellulose one, as it gives a very smooth effect. Professional marblers generally use this. If possible, mix it up a few hours or even the night before use.

CARAGHEEN

Alternatively, you can get some excellent results with a bath made of caragheen (Irish moss), which is made from a kind of seaweed. This is a rather more fiddly procedure as the bath has to be made the day before you want to marble.

To make up the bath, add a little cold water to one dessertspoonful of caragheen powder. Now beat it into a thick paste with an electric whisk or a blender, add 1.4 litres (2¼ pints) of hot water and carry on blending for about five minutes, until it resembles egg white. Repeat the process if you need more to fill your bath – it should be about 5cm (2in) deep.

Now let the caragheen stand overnight before using it, protecting it with some sort of dust cover. When it is ready to use (at least twelve hours later), virtually all the bubbles will have disappeared.

The next day, remember to skim the surface of the bath with newspaper before you start marbling.

A LARGER BATH

You may also now want to use a bigger size of bath, and now that you have had sufficient practice in marbling you may feel competent to do so. Garden centres have large plastic plant trays (they must be 7.5mm (3in) in depth) and caterers' suppliers and photographic shops also sell various deep trays and containers.

Also, large, strong cardboard boxes from the supermarket can be lined with plastic sheeting or an old shower curtain, so that it is possible to have several different-sized baths.

This Japanese wallet by Polly Fox demonstrates the clear, sharp patterns obtainable on a caragheen bath.

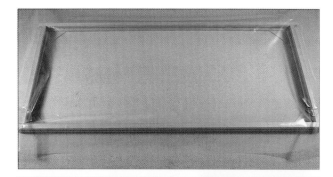

USING AN EXTRA-LARGE BATH

If you want a really large or long bath, you could make your own.

1 Construct a strong wooden frame, either with or without a base, and line it with thick plastic sheeting. It need not be very deep: in fact the deeper it is the longer it will take to fill and empty.

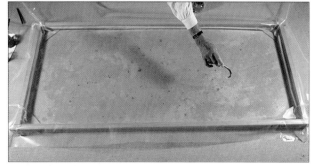

2 Fill the bath in the usual way and add the colours in whatever pattern you wish.

3 If your fabric is very long, tack it at the ends on to wooden rods, to make it easier to put down. If someone helps you, the procedure will be even simpler. Lay the fabric down carefully and evenly, letting the middle of the fabric touch the surface of the bath first.

4 You can marble quite large pieces of fabric using this method. The big disadvantage of this size of bath is that it must be emptied by hand, which can be quite a lengthy and messy process!

MARBLING DIFFICULT SHAPES

When marbling T-shirts or shorts, you should either pad the article out with rolled-up newspaper or else insert a strong piece of card cut to fit in it before rolling it over in the bath. All this takes a little practice, so it is better to start off with small articles.

While squares of material will not be a problem, you may find that a scarf or tie is too long for your bath. The tie can be folded longways over a piece of card and then turned over in the bath. The card protects the unmarbled side from getting wet, because if it did it would not take the marbling properly.

Another answer is shown below, using a cardboard roll.

1 Roll the scarf or tie round the cardboard centre of a roll of kitchen or lavatory paper.

2 Unroll sufficient of the tie to fit easily the length of the bath and lay down that part of it on to the surface of the bath.

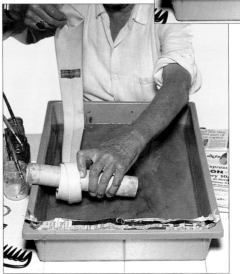

3 Unroll more of the unmarbled part and lay this down on a part of the bath from which no film of colour has yet been taken up, taking care to marble up to the join with no gap or overlap. Continue until the whole tie is marbled all over.

ADDITIVES

As you have already found, fabric paints have an additive which makes them float on the surface when diluted with water. There are other substances which can also be added, either as well as or in place of water, which can create different and interesting results. Since these additives are all very powerful, and must be added in minute quantities to your paints, it is advisable to put them in tiny squeezy bottles, or small eye-dropper bottles, so that a few drops can be added at a time.

WASHING-UP LIQUID

Washing-up liquid is the most easily available. It is a good idea to add this to one colour only, if you are using three or four, and to let it be the last one you put down. You will find that it makes the other colours disperse and form into smaller, darker shapes. You can also splatter diluted washing-up liquid on to your bath when all the colours have been put down, which creates a different effect.

The effect of adding an additive on top of a marbled pattern – large clear areas allow the original colour of the fabric to come through.

ACRYLIC-BASED EXTENDER MEDIUM

An acrylic-based extender medium can be used to dilute your colour, using equal parts of colour and extender, and one or two parts water as needed to make your colour fluid. Since less water is used, your colours will be deeper. You can buy this medium at art shops.

MARBLING MEDIUM

Marbling medium, or marbleising liquid, is a special commercial substance which can be used in place of water to dilute your colours. This, too, can be found at art shops.

PHOTOGRAPHIC WETTING AGENT

Photographic wetting agent is another substance, like detergent, which acts as a surfactant – *i.e.* breaks up the surface tension of the bath and causes the colours to spread. You can add it directly to the colour, either instead of, or with, a little water, until the colours are diluted.

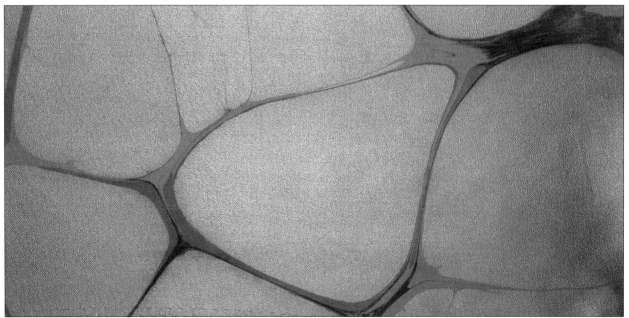

MARBLING WITH ACRYLICS

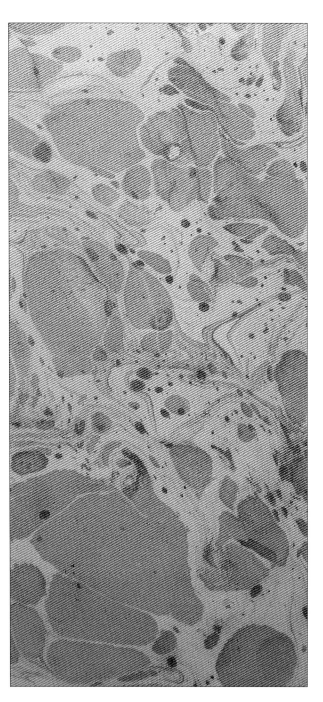

This method of marbling is exactly as described in previous chapters, but we are using acrylic paints instead of fabric paints, which gives us a much wider range of colour. The paints are widely used by professional marblers, as they float naturally, making them particularly suitable for marbling.

Again you should mix the colours to the consistency of thin cream, using one of the following methods:

1. Dilute with water

2. Dilute with equal parts of acrylic extender medium and water

3. Dilute with a proprietary brand of marbling medium

Prepare your fabric with an alum solution, and then use the colours in the usual way, floating them on the surface of the bath.

Since each colour is made with different pigments, the performance of each can vary a little. Some of the colours work consistently well, others can be less successful. A basic selection of six to eight colours will be enough to start with, and the following work consistently well: burnt sienna, brilliant yellow, permanent alizarin crimson hue, phthalocyanine green, ultramarine blue, dioxazine purple, prism violet, cerulean blue, turquoise green, and deep magenta.

The paints are water-soluble, so brushes and pots can be cleaned as before with hot water and detergent.

Left and opposite: acrylics on cotton.

MARBLING WITH OIL PAINTS

Again, this method of marbling is exactly the same as that described in *How to begin*. The difference here is in the paints used: instead of fabric paints, oil paints (such as tubes of students' oils) are used. You simply dilute them with turpentine or spirits of turpentine to make them liquid enough to drop on to the surface of your bath.

The advantage of oil paints over fabric paints or acrylics is that the material does not have to be pre-washed, if new, or soaked in an alum solution to mordant it. The colours are strong, and the fabric will feel stiffer, with a more brocade-like effect. With oil paints you can also marble fabric which will not easily accept fabric paints or acrylics, such as dark-coloured materials, felt, or even pale leather.

The main disadvantage is that since the colours are oil-based and not water-soluble, cleaning up after your marbling is a much messier business, because it has to be done with turpentine, not water. It helps if you collect a lot of small plastic yoghurt pots to mix your paint in, because they can then be thrown away after use. (Do not, however, use disposable polystyrene cups, because the turpentine which dilutes your colours also dissolves the cups, with disastrous results!)

It is also a good idea to line your bath with aluminium foil, to protect it, and throw it away when you have finished.

A pile of old rags for wiping your hands with turpentine to keep them clean is essential. If you find that turpentine irritates your skin, then wear gloves or use a barrier cream.

Most manufacturers of artists' oil colours also produce a range for students, which work perfectly well and will be cheaper. Also, instead of buying turpentine to dissolve your colours and to clean up with, you can buy turpentine substitute, which is also far cheaper than pure turpentine. Do not, however, buy very cheap white spirit, because it is too unrefined. It also has a very strong smell.

For your bath, methyl cellulose wallpaper paste gives a much smoother result than ordinary cellulose wallpaper paste, and is worth seeking out in DIY shops or builders' merchants'.

The preparation of the work surface and your bath will be as before: only the mixing of the colours will be different.

To start with, buy tubes of the primary colours – blue, red and yellow – and one of black. For the blue, coeruleum blue is very good, and there is a very pretty colour called rose madder (a dark pinky-red) which is preferable to the cadmium red for mixing with other colours. A clear chrome yellow and any of the blacks make up the rest.

To start mixing, squeeze 6mm (¼in) of paint into the pot you are going to use. Then slowly, drop by drop, add the turpentine or turpentine substitute to it, mixing very carefully with your brush until the oil paint is quite dissolved.

When it is absolutely smooth and free from lumps, add a little more turpentine to make it liquid enough to drop freely from your brush. If you are mixing two colours together, make sure they are evenly and smoothly mixed before adding too much turpentine, otherwise it will be very difficult and time-consuming to get the little lumps out, and your colour will be grainy.

To start marbling, test out your colours in the bath. If you find that they do not spread satisfactorily, or if they sink, add a little more turpentine and try again. If they spread too much, add a little more paint very carefully and make sure it is thoroughly dissolved.

Oils on silk.

Oils on synthetic fabric.

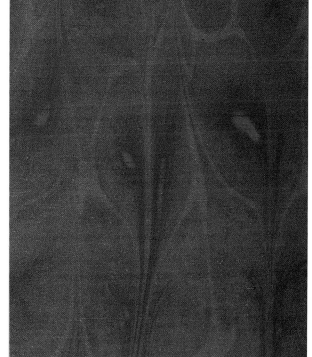

Oils on polyester.

Oils on heavy silk.

Oils on cotton.

You will also find that some oil colours are stronger than others, and by changing the order in which you drop them on the surface of the bath, you can also change the effect. It is worth experimenting.

When you have done all this, you are ready to start marbling as before.

If, when you take up the marbled fabric from the bath, you find that the 'slime' from the bath is adhering to it, wash this off gently with cold water.

Otherwise you do not have to rinse oil-marbled fabric; simply lay it flat on newsprint to dry off, or hang it up.

When working with oils, do not use the same brushes and tools that you use for marbling with fabric paints or acrylics, as any remaining trace of oil or turpentine will affect your colours and prevent them from working satisfactorily.

MORE IDEAS

ONE-COLOUR MARBLING

You will find that some fabrics, however, look better marbled in one colour only, and if this colour is applied gently but generously all over the surface, almost covering it, and then swirled, it can make a truly 'marbled' effect which is very attractive.

OVER-MARBLING

Marble your fabric once, let it dry, iron it quite smooth, and then marble on top of the original pattern.

FLOWERS

Creative use of your stylus can produce some wonderful patterns, such as this flower by Elizabeth Vreeland (used on her quilt on page 34). Carefully pull the paint into the required shape in a controlled manner, using your stylus.

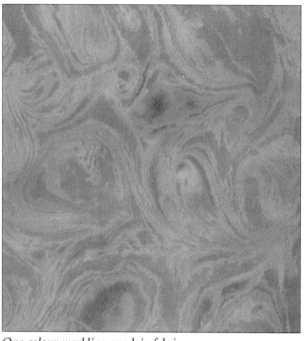

One-colour marbling on plain fabric.

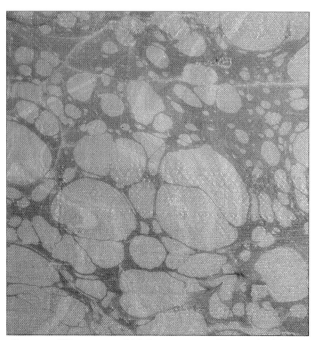

Over-marbling: grey pebbled pattern over blue and white.

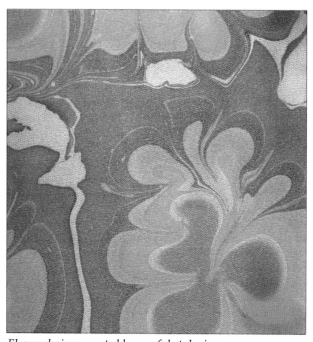

Flower designs created by careful stylusing.

MARBLING PROBLEMS

I do not think any experienced marbler would claim that this is an exact science, and that every day will produce brilliant work – it can be quite erratic. However, there are certain problems which can be recurrent, and it is useful to recognise them, so that they can be dealt with.

It is worth taking a little time, and giving some thought to your problem, rather than keep marbling on, hoping it will adjust itself. Look at your bath first, since if there is a problem there, that will be the easiest fault to spot.

THE BATH

If the bath is too thick, the colour will not spread satisfactorily, so check this and add some warm water to dilute it if necessary. If the bath is too thin, you will have trouble controlling the colours, so add some more thick size to the bath and mix it well.

If the bath has become saturated and muddy with colour, it will be difficult to get clear impressions on the fabric, so it is better to throw the bath away and start again. If, however, the surplus colour is simply on the surface, using thick kitchen paper instead of newspaper to clean it off often works.

THE COLOURS

Rather more things can go wrong with colours: try to analyse what is wrong first of all.

If the colours are not spreading, and you have checked that the bath is neither too thick nor too cold, then you must either dilute the colours further or add more surfactant to make them spread. Try one, and then the other.

If the colours spread too much, then you have probably added too *much* surfactant. Mix some fresh colour in a separate pot, then slowly add the original colour to it until you have adjusted the balance.

If the colours spread, but then splinter or become star-shaped, this is usually because the surface tension of the bath has built up and is preventing the colours from spreading naturally. Either you should skim the surface of the bath more carefully with your strip of newspaper, or else (and this is a common problem) you are working too slowly and allowing the surface tension to build up before you have put down your paints.

If your colours are 'grainy', or contain little blobs, it is usually because you did not mix them well enough before you added all the liquid (water, turpentine, or whatever). If you seem to have an excess of colour on your fabric, rinse it gently but thoroughly in cold water before hanging it up to dry.

If your colours appear streaky on the fabric, it may be because you have not mordanted it thoroughly or evenly.

RESCUING FAILURES BY OVER-MARBLING

If you have used, for example, a precious piece of silk, and failed to marble it as satisfactorily as you had hoped, you can let it dry, iron it quite smooth, and then either remarble on top of the original, or marble on the other side. The effect can be surprisingly good.

You can also get a pretty result by marbling ribbons as bookmarks in this way, with each side different. (See the double-marbled silk handkerchief on page 47.)

If you leave a bubble of air on the surface of your bath the fabric will not pick up the colour where the bubble appears.

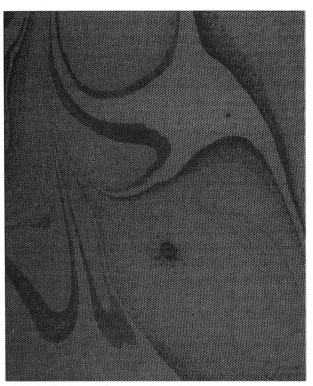

A blob of paint – take care when mixing.

The pattern on this fabric dominates the marbling, which does not show up sufficiently for a good balance.

There was not really enough colour on the bath when this piece of fabric was laid down.

GALLERY

Colour Fantasy *quilt by Elizabeth Vreeland.*

ELIZABETH A. VREELAND
Syracuse, America

Elizabeth, who has a degree in surface pattern design, has been marbling and teaching marbling for three years. She particularly enjoys making beautiful quilts in silk, cotton and polyester.

This sampler quilt, *Colour Fantasy* (100 x 110cm (40in x 44in)), is made up of a wide variety of combed patterns and flower designs, edged with a feathery toning border. She marbled the 12.5cm (5in) squares of white polyester satin in a new 22.5 x 30cm (9 x 12in) aluminium roasting tin, using acrylic paints on a methyl cellulose bath. The pieces were then machine-sewn together and the quilting finished by hand.

Opposite: detail of quilt.

KOJO TATSUNO

Japan, France and England

A dress designer who is deeply interested in unusual fabrics, he marbled lengths of chiffon and silk for these beautiful clothes which were shown in Paris in the 1994 spring/summer collections.

Photographs by Andrew Lamb.

A stunning fashionable gown with a spattered pattern in blue, beige and lilac.

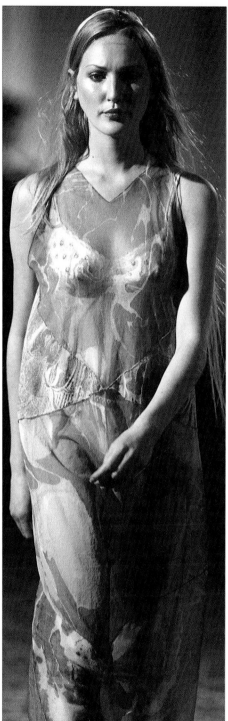

*A diaphanous chiffon gown with
a large pattern in subtle colours.*

*Left: a two-tone pattern on
silk creates a dramatic effect.*

37

POLLY FOX
America

Polly Fox, a professional marbler on paper and fabric, publishes and edits *Ink and Gall*, a tri-annual review of marbling with a world-wide circulation. She has also published her own book on the subject.

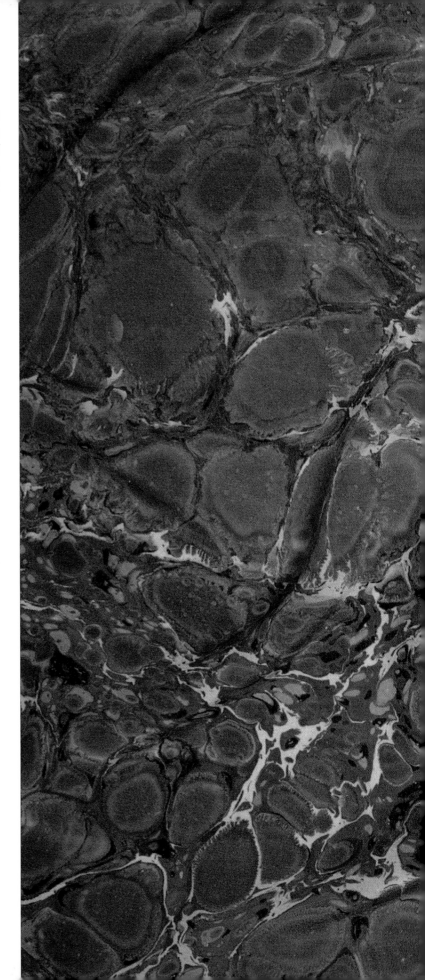

Crepe-de-chine silk scarf by Polly Fox, marbled with acrylic colours on a caragheen bath.

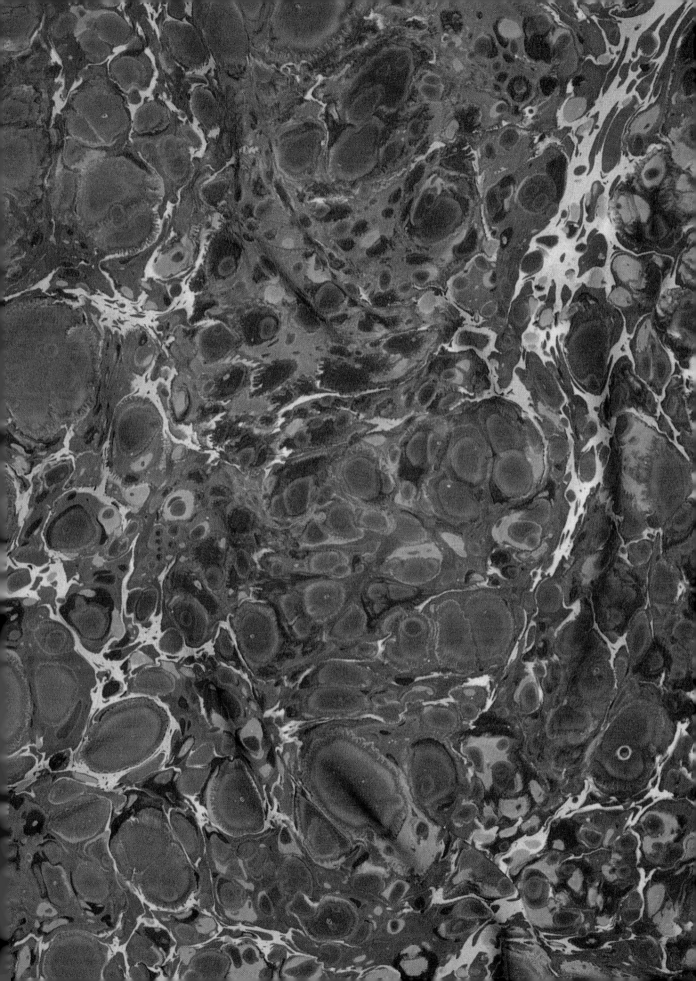

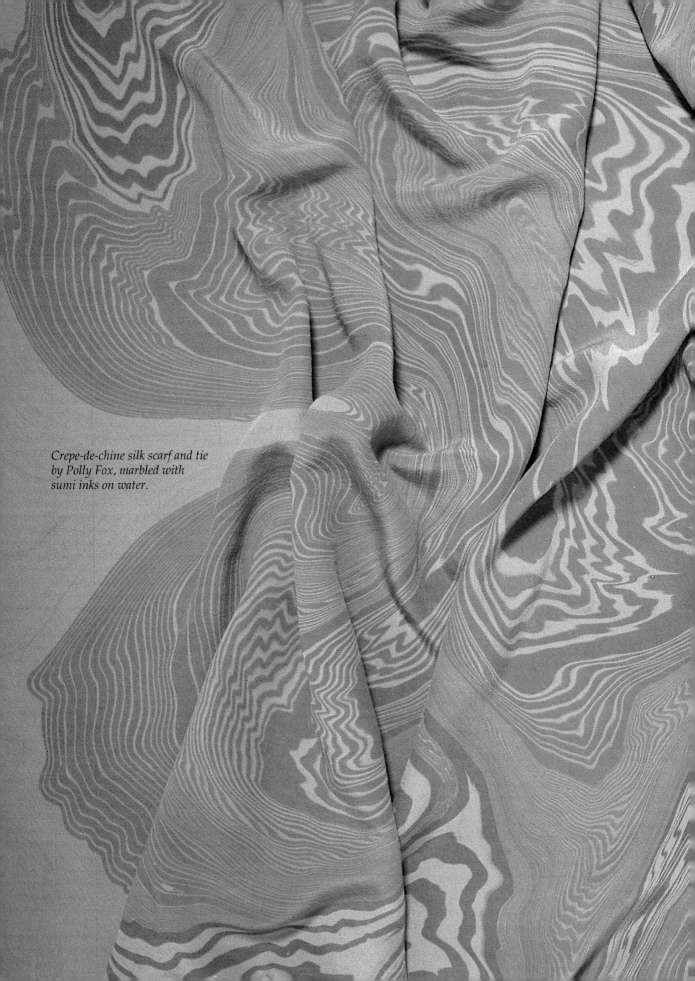

Crepe-de-chine silk scarf and tie by Polly Fox, marbled with sumi inks on water.

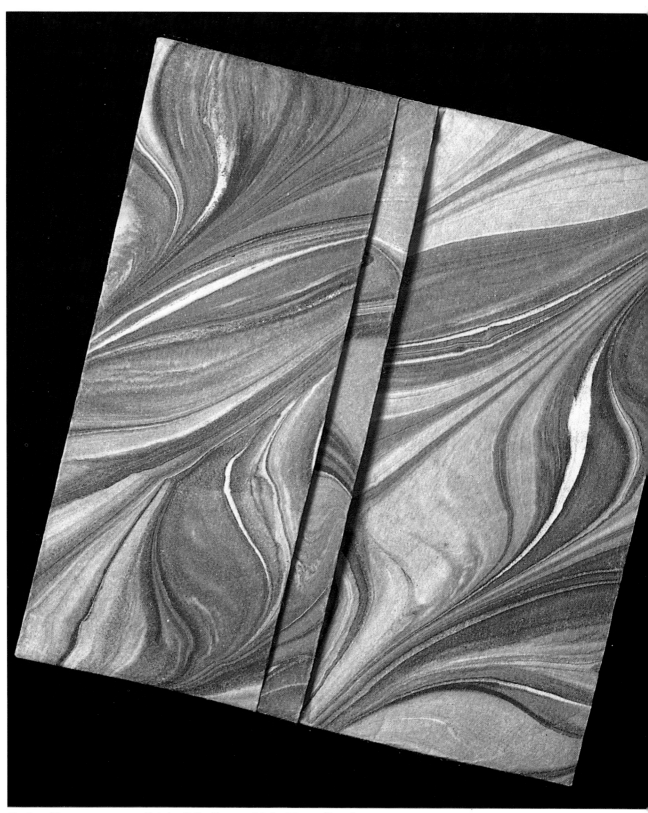

Copies of Japanese paper wallets by Polly Fox, marbled with acrylic colours on pelon, using a caragheen bath.

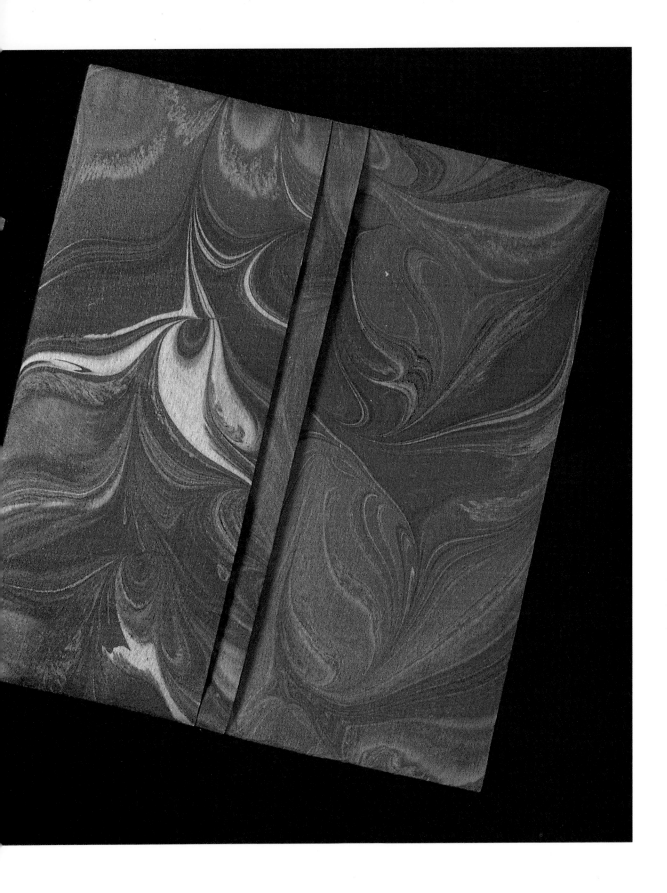

Cotton fabric for quilters, by Polly Fox, marbled with acrylics on a bath of caragheen.

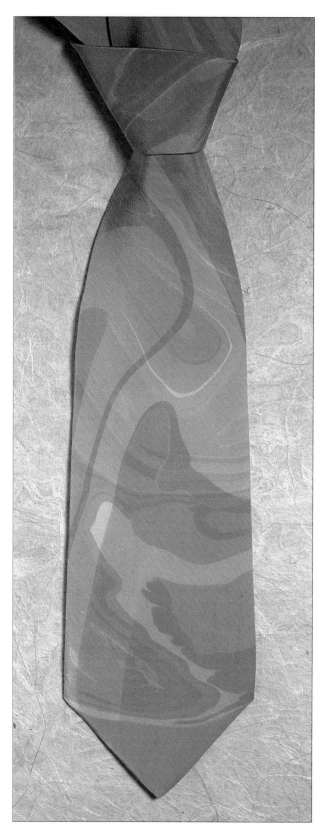

Silk tie by Polly Fox.

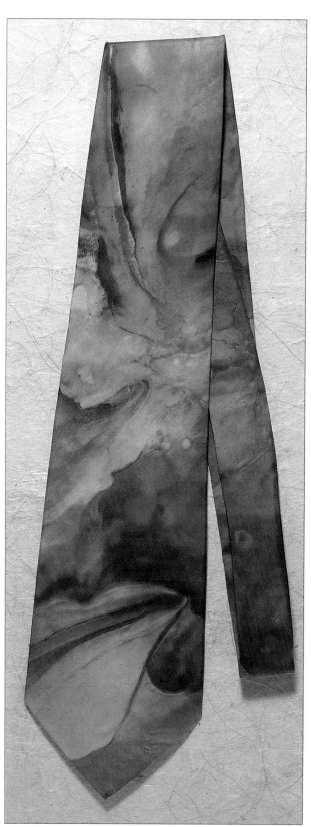

Marbled silk tie from Turkey.

VICTORIA HALL

England

A well-known professional marbler, she produces regular designs and recreates antiquarian pattern styles for bookbinders using traditional methods. However, she also loves exploring other methods of marbling, and marbled these plain white espadrilles using oil colours on a methyl cellulose bath. They were dipped in pairs to ensure a good match, and keeping the pattern even, the insides clean and the rope soles dry needed a little thought and steady hands.

FRANÇOISE COMACLE
France

Françoise has been a professional marbler for seventeen years. She marbles on paper, fabric, leather, wood and candles, using watercolour, acrylic or oil paints on a bath of powdered caragheen moss. She has also made rich brocade-like fabrics for films such as *Cyrano de Bergerac*.

BIBLIOGRAPHY

Fabric Marbling: Iris Nevens. Published by Iris Nevens, Sussex, New Jersey, U.S.A.

Marbling on Fabric: Polly Fox. Fresh Ink Press, Taos, New Mexico 87571, U.S.A.

Marbling on Fabric: Daniel & Paula Cohen. Interweave Press, U.S.A.

Marbling on Paper with Oil Paints: Anne Chambers. Search Press Ltd., Tunbridge Wells, England.

INDEX